Thomas Ewing

Speech of Maj. Gen. Thomas Ewing, Jr., of Kansas : made before the National Delegate Convention of Union Soldiers and Sailors at Cooper Institute, New York, July 4, 1868

Thomas Ewing

Speech of Maj. Gen. Thomas Ewing, Jr., of Kansas : made before the National Delegate Convention of Union Soldiers and Sailors at Cooper Institute, New York, July 4, 1868

ISBN/EAN: 9783337305574

Printed in Europe, USA, Canada, Australia, Japan

Cover: Foto ©ninafisch / pixelio.de

More available books at **www.hansebooks.com**

SPEECH

OF

MAJ. GEN. THOMAS EWING, JR.,

OF KANSAS,

MADE BEFORE THE

NATIONAL DELEGATE CONVENTION

OF

UNION SOLDIERS AND SAILORS,

AT

COOPER INSTITUTE, NEW YORK,

July 4, 1868.

REPORTED AND PUBLISHED BY ORDER OF THE CONVENTION.

SPEECH

OF

MAJ. GEN. THOMAS EWING, Jr.,

OF KANSAS,

AT THE

SOLDIERS' AND SAILORS' NATIONAL CONVENTION,

AT

COOPER INSTITUTE,

JULY 4, 1868.

REPORTED AND PUBLISHED BY ORDER OF THE CONVENTION.

Mr. President and Gentlemen of the Convention:

I heartily thank you for the honor of being called upon to address this vast assemblage of soldiers and sailors—the largest ever gathered on the continent since the grand review in Washington, at the close of the war, of the victorious armies of the Potomac, of the Tennessee, and of Georgia. Of the comrades who separated then, and went each to his home and civic occupation, almost every regiment has here its representative. Why have we, soldiers and sailors, who are proud of our service for the Union, assembled here in delegate convention to plan the overthrow of that political party which administered the Government through the war, and the defeat for the Presidency of him who was erst the leader of the Union armies? (Applause.) With your indulgence, I will endeavor briefly to give the reasons for our meeting, and our intended action. (Cries of "Go on.")

On the 4th of July, three years ago, the war for the suppression of the rebellion had wholly ended. General Lee had surrendered to General Grant the Army of Northern Virginia, and its officers and men were plowing the fields of the Old Dominion, drenched with the blood and scorched by the fires of four years of devastating war. Joe Johnston had surrendered to Sherman (applause) the daring and stubborn troops which our Western army had driven inch by inch from Belmont to Raleigh; and Shelby's frontier command were scattered over the hemisphere from Montana to Brazil. (Laughter.) There was not in arms a Confederate soldier, mounted or on foot; not a dockyard, fort, or arsenal, in which there was a rebel ship, cannon, or musket; not a rood of land on earth, or a foot of deck on sea, over which a Confederate banner waved. The last rebel privateers were being dragged for condemnation from the Indian Ocean and the North Pacific; and the haughtiest leaders of the rebellion were wandering outcast over the earth, or seeking pardon of a President who was a noble type at once of the loyal Southerner they had hated, and the laboring white man they had despised. (Applause.) Never was there a rebellion more utterly overthrown, or a cause more hopelessly lost.

The people of the Southern States, with wonderful promptness, quiet, and unanimity, submitted to the result. You all know it was commonly predicted and believed, North and South, that when the great armies of the Confederacy were conquered, dispersing, they would fill the land with guerrillas, and wage a Vendean warfare more destructive and irrepressible than the regular war out of which it grew. But this prediction was not in the smallest degree verified. Within sixty days after the last great battle of the war, the Federal marshals and tax-gatherers executed their processes unarmed and unattended throughout the Southern States, in the jungles lately swarming with guerrillas, and over fields lately shaken with the roar of rebel artillery. The whole people of the South *bowed to the authority of the nation*, with hearts in which, as they were human, there were yet doubtless revenges and sorrows, humiliations and bereavements, and undying attachments to the cause they had dearly loved and bravely maintained, but which yielded implicitly all that the people, the President, or the war party had ever told them were the purposes of the war. And by the Constitutional Conventions and Legislatures, chosen by the electors of the Southern States the year the rebellion ended, their several constitutions and statutes were amended, abolishing slavery and the harsh codes founded on it, abandoning the doctrine of secession, repudiating the rebel debt, recognizing the national debt, and, in short, giving every guaranty which men could give, that in a spirit of concord they recognized and accepted, as accomplished, every avowed object of the war.

Now, the Republican party was bound, in loyalty, honor, and good conscience, to accept this submission, and at once restore the Union by admitting the Southern States to representation, so far as they presented senators and representatives personally qualified. (Applause.) It was bound to do it, out of obedience to the Constitution, in the sacred name of which the war was waged, and which, while allowing each House to judge of the qualifications of its own members, prohibits the exclusion from representation of any State *as a State*. And it was bound to do it, because the war was avowedly waged for the sole purpose of effecting the unconditional restoration of the Union, immediately upon the unconditional submission of the Southern people, through amendments of their constitutions and laws, to the national authority. Said Sherman to the South, in his Atlanta letter:

"We don't want your negroes or your horses, your houses or your lands, or any thing you have; we only want, and will have, a just obedience to the Constitution and laws of the United States." (Applause.) And in that declaration he expressed the sole purpose of the war as declared by the Government, and understood by the army and navy and people of the Union. The Republican party, in its National Convention in 1864—just after Horace Greeley had tried to effect a dishonorable peace through George N. Sanders and Beverly Tucker (hisses and laughter)—declared that the war was, and should be waged only, to force "an unconditional surrender of hostility by the rebels, and a return to their just allegiance to the Constitution and laws of the United States." And from the beginning to the close of the war, there stood, and still stands, on our statute books, a law declaring that the war should be waged "in no spirit of oppression, but solely to restore the Union with all the dignity, equality, and rights of the several States unimpaired." (Applause.) That law was the pledge of the Republican party made in 1861, and reiterated in National Convention in 1864, that the tremendous powers confided to it by the people, without regard to party, for the vindication of the national authority, should never be used for party or sectional dominion. And on the faith of that pledge were given every dollar of money and every drop of blood spent in the war. (Applause.)

But the Republican party had not the wisdom or patriotism to accept this submission of the Southern people, and promptly restore the Union. It recollected that before the war it was a minority party, and came into power, in 1861, through a division of the Democratic party, by much less than half the popular vote. Yet, with the prestige and moral power resulting from a successful prosecution of the war, nd a prompt and cordial restoration of the Union, it could have retained power until this generation of voters had passed away or had forgotten the anti-war follies of the Democratic party. But it took counsel of its fears, doubted its own destiny, forgot the inextinguishable love in the hearts of the Northern people for the Constitution and the Union, and therefore refused to take what the war was alone waged to get—a prompt and cordial pacification and reunion under the Constitution. It did this in the vain hope of controlling the Southern States by making voters of the negroes, and proscribing all the intelligent white men whom Congress and the Freedman's Bureau could not bribe, or coax, or kick, or cuff into Republicanism. But while destroying the ten Southern States, and building in their stead ten rotten boroughs, to be represented in Congress in the interests of the Northern radicals by white adventurers and plantation negroes, the party is losing its strong hold on the *Northern* States, and, like the dog in the fable, drops the substance to snatch at the shadow. (Laughter and applause.)

The first step toward postponing reunion until the Southern States could be subjugated by the radical party, It was the offer, in 1866, of the Constitutional amendment. It contained declarations of the results of the war, which the Southern States had already inserted in their constitutions and codes under the advice of President Johnson, and to which they freely assented; and an alternative of negro suffrage or reduction of representation, and also important additions to the power of the Federal Government, to which they would have assented reluctantly for the sake of reunion. But, inseparably coupled with these, and making with them one proposition, which had to be accepted or rejected as a whole, was the clause of disfranchisement, which they could not accept without dishonor. It disqualified from holding any office, petty or exalted, *State or Federal*, in effect, every man who was of age when the war broke out and was fit to hold any office. So sweeping was the proposed proscription, that, after it was adopted into the reconstruction acts, Generals Meade, Schofield, and Canby successively reported that it was impossible to administer the governments of the Southern States while enforcing it, because, in many communities, there was really not a man fit to hold any office who was not disqualified by it. The Southern people did as the radical leaders wished and knew they would—rejected the amendment. They acted like men in doing so. (Applause.) Let us ask ourselves, gentlemen, whether, if the North had rebelled and been conquered, and the South had offered us reunion on condition that we should ourselves vote to disfranchise and degrade every Northern man who could read and write and cipher to the rule of three, as punishment for the rebellion in which all had participated, and to commit the government and destinies of our States to the hands of only the most ignorant of our people, or to the camp-followers of the conquering army, *we* would have voted for our own disgrace and disfranchisement? (Voices, "No, no.") No people who are fit to be free would thus with their own hands put on their own necks the yoke of political slavery. (Great applause.) And so far from the rejection of that clause and the proposed amendment of the Constitution with which it was inseparably connected, being a just cause of complaint against the Southern people, they would have merited the scorn and contempt of all high-minded men had they accepted it.

But the amendment served its purpose in the campaign of 1866. It was, to the careless or superficial observer, an effort in good faith by the radical party to effect reunion. The Southern legislatures, unanimously and promptly, but respectfully, declared that they could not accept it ; and were therefore violently denounced by the radical press and orators, as still defiant and rebellious. Just then, the most mischievous men of both parties in New Orleans contrived to bring on a bloody riot ; and the radicals rode the tempest it created, and swept the North.

Since then, with three-fourths of both Houses of Congress on their side, and animated by a thorough contempt of the Constitution, the radical party has been omnipotent. It has protracted disunion nearly as long as the rebels did—and done more to destroy our form of Government than all the parties that ever controlled its destines.

On the 8th of July, 1863, in a debate in the House of Representatives, Old Thad Stevens (hisses) bluntly and boldly announced the doctrine that the Southern States were not States of the Union, and that Congress could legislate over them as over conquered territory. If this doctrine be true, it is because the acts of secession were constitutional, and in legal effect took the States out of the Union—that is, that under the Constitution, the States had a right to secede, and, therefore the United States had no right to make war on them for seceding. This rebel doctrine, when thus announced by Stevens, was violently assailed by Owen Lovejoy, and other fierce radicals of the House, and repudiated in the name of the war party.

In the year following, in the National Union Convention at Baltimore, Stevens again proclaimed this doctrine, declaring that Tennessee was but a subject province, and Andrew Johnson an alien enemy. But the Convention contemptuously repudiated his theory, and gave emphasis to its declaration by nominating Mr. Johnson for Vice-President, and indorsing Mr. Lincoln's reconstruction policy. All this, however, was while the war was going on, and while soldiers were being called for to fight in the holy cause of the Constitution and the Union, and not for conquest. (Applause.) But when the rebellion ended, and the elections of 1866 gave the radicals a new lease of power, this infamous dogma, which, if true, makes the war for secession Constitutional and just, and the war for the Union a wicked and unprovoked conquest—a doctrine, which three years before had been, like the hateful Richard—

> "Sent before its time,
> Into this breathing world, scarce half made up,
> And that so lamely and unfashionable,
> That dogs barked at it as it halted by them,"

was now adopted by the Republican party as the fundamental theory of reconstruction and the shibboleth of loyalty.

Having fully adopted this rebel theory that the Southern States were out of the Union, and unsheltered by the broad ægis of the Constitution, Congress declared invalid the governments chosen by the electors of those States under the advice of Presidents Lincoln and Johnson, in conformity with State constitutions and laws, and established over them military dictatorships, through which to inaugurate the rule of the negroes and their Northern allies. But here a new rent in their programme was discovered, requiring to be patched by a newly-invented dogma. The Calhoun-Stevens theory of the validity of secession was good as far as it stretched; but, like a shelter tent, was neither broad nor long enough. It took the States out, and made them conquered provinces, but did not increase the power of Congress, nor deprive the inhabitants of the conquered territory of those guaranties of life, liberty, and property which the Constitution extends *to citizens and aliens alike* on every foot of ground within the jurisdiction of the United States—the right of exemption from punishment by *ex post facto* laws; the liberty of speech and of the press; the right to keep and bear arms; the right to be free from unreasonable searches and seizures, and from deprivation of life, liberty, or property without due process of law; the right of trial by jury; and, above all, the privilege of the writ of *habeas corpus*—that shield of liberty, in possession of which the people of a monarchy are free, and without which a Republic is a despotism. (Great applause.) These constitutional guaranties were in the way of coercive reconstruction ; and Congress was forbidden, in peace, to touch any one of them. Unless these ancient and sacred liberties could be destroyed, vigorous military despotisms could not be established—and without such despotisms, radical reconstruction was impossible. While these guaranties remained in the Constitution, and were obeyed, the whole governing talent of the South could not be disfranchised by a sweeping *ex post facto* law : Governors of States duly chosen by the electors in accordance with State constitutions and laws could not be removed by district commanders as impediments to reconstruction ; State legislatures could not be prorogued at the point of the bayonet ; State treasuries could not be robbed, and widow and orphan creditors defrauded of their dividends to pay plantation negroes eight dollars a day for making constitutions (Applause.) New codes of laws, framed by Solons and moralists like Dan Sickles (hisses), could not be proclaimed and enforced over the Carolinas ; a Judge conducting a murder trial could not be pushed from the bench, and the trial carried on to conviction, sentence, and execution, by a colonel in uniform ; American citizens —citizens of one of the original thirteen States, charged with no crime, could not be arrested by scores, on *lettres de cachet* signed by a post-adjutant, immured in loathsome dungeons, and tortured to the point of death with the boot and sweat box, to make them swear to what a military commander *suspected* they knew touching the murder of some wretch like Ashburn (applause) ; and military commissions, those courts, organized to convict, at whose doors no man can lay a charge of uncertainty as to the law, or doubt or delay or undue clemency in its execution, which adopt the efficient rule that it is better that ninety-nine innocent men should be punished, than one guilty man escape, could not inspire respect for the radical party and its measures by being prepared at a moment's warning to try any citizen for any act, which in the opinion of the officer convening the court, was a " crime against reconstruction," and to sentence him for months, or years, or life, to the dungeon or the Dry Tortugas, beyond the reach of Executive pardon or reprieve.

It was indispensable, therefore to get rid of these constitutional provisions, which are at once guaranties of the liberties of the people, and prohibitions of power to Congress. To avoid an avowal of a purpose to trample on the Constitution, the party, with decent hypocrisy, claimed a new derivation of Congressional power. They said that a formidable rebellion was never contemplated by the framers of the Constitution, and no powers were conferred in anticipation of such an emergency. Congress, therefore, was compelled, in the matter of reconstruction, to act *outside of the Constitution.*

The framers of the Constitution were the sons and grandsons of the Puritans and the Cavaliers who kept England smoking with civil wars for half a century (applause) : and who knew by personal experience how despotic was power when inflamed by the passions of domestic war—whether that power were the legitimate Sovereign, the Pretender, or Parliament. And with recollections of this recent English history, and traditions of family persecutions, fresh in their minds—anticipating that the bold spirit of their sons would be transmitted to their children, and break out in occasional revolts against the national authority—the framers of the Constitution not only withheld from Congress the power of inflicting, in peace punishments at will for political offenses, but also inserted those guaranties of personal liberty *ex industria*, as express prohibitions, in order to prevent a Congress driving the people to renewed war, or to flight by measures of revenge such as sent their forefathers from England to our shores. (Great applause.)

As to Congress deriving power in any contingency outside of the Constitution, it is enough to say that Congress gets all its powers from the Constitution, and outside of it has no powers, and *is no Congress* (applause) : and that all its acts not authorized by the Constitution, are mere usurpations, whether against express prohibitions or not. If you present this argument to radicals, they will reply that the Constitution in not giving Congress such authority, is therein defective, and Congress needs, and must exercise it. A French philosopher once propounded to Professor Faraday, a new theory of the transmission of light : which the English philosopher heard patiently and then objected to it, that the theory was inconsistent with certain established facts of natural science. "So much ze worse for ze *facts*," was the ready answer of the confident Frenchman. So, if you prove the reconstruction plan unconstitutional, the radicals, in effect, answer, "So much the worse for the *Constitution*." (Great applause.)

Thus, to secure a reconstruction giving the radicals of the North absolute control of the ten States of the South, not only were the State governments abolished and military despotisms built on their ruins, but every revered guaranty of life, liberty, and property, which the Southern people and ourselves inherited from a free ancestry, and which our forefathers and their forefathers placed in the Constitution to be beyond the reach of the rude hand of faction, was boldly destroyed. No civilized people on this earth are as wholly without legal protection from the capricious oppression of their rulers as the Southern people under these military despotisms. It is amazing how passively the people, North and South, have borne this gross, dangerous, insolent usurpation. But it has been quietly submitted to because of the belief—

now, thank God! almost certainty—that the Northern people will, in November, seize this radical party and its half-executed usurpations, and dash them to pieces (prolonged cheering); and because many of the military commanders have tempered the harsh rule they were sent to inflict out of that love for our ancient liberties which is born in every true American, and which so shone through the administration of at least one of those commanders as to cover with new and fadeless glory the twice-illustrious name of Hancock. (Tumultuous cheering and waving of hats.)

Gentlemen, I do not understand how any white American, proud of our race and of our free systems of government, can behold, without mingled disgust and indignation, the methods and results of Congressional reconstruction, and the pretenses by which it is sustained. It is claimed to be in the interests of *peace*—while fomenting deadly strife and rancor between the two races, arraying them into conflicting parties, subjecting the superior to the inferior, and then leaving them to struggle for dominion! In the interest of *liberty* and *progress*—while tearing down ten free, enlightened States, four of the old thirteen that founded the Republic, and establishing in their stead ten despotisms, in which the intelligent and cultivated white man is made subject to the ignorant and brutal negro—despotisms mitigated only by the fact that the negroes are but the *ostensible* rulers of the Southern whites, while the Northern radicals are the *real* ones that the negro acts only the part of the *automaton chessplayer*, while the Northern radical party is the unseen intellect which directs the senseless hand that fingers the pawns. It is claimed to be in the interests of *national prosperity*—while wasting the wealth and paralyzing the industries of the South on the one hand, and doubling the burdens of the Northern taxpayers and destroying the eager markets for their manufactures and breadstuffs on the other. What a spectacle for gods and men does not this reconstruction present! See the black laborers of the South, fed in idleness out of moneys wrung from the toil of Northern white men (applause), filled with ambition to rule the whites, and to grow rich by confiscations, and becoming each year more utterly and irreclaimably idle and thriftless. The splendid sugar, cotton, and rice plantations, at once the evidence and the product of a century of civilization, overgrown with weeds; idle machinery rusting in the sugar-houses; the floods of the Mississippi sweeping over neglected levees and abandoned plantations, and the boorish negro field-hands sitting in conventions! Behold Virginia, the Niobe of States, the mother of Presidents and illustrious statesmen—her at whose call our great free Republic was formed—her by whose free gift the Republic acquired the territory of the six great States of the Northwest! See the civil government founded by her Washington (applause), Madison (applause), Jefferson (applause), Lee (applause), the foremost statesmen of their day on the earth, destroyed, supplanted by a military despotism, and that, in turn, about to be supplanted by a civil government framed by infamous whites like Hunnicutt, and a rabble of half-civilized negroes (hisses). If this be prosperity, progress, and liberty, God send us misfortune, reaction, and despotism forever! (Prolonged applause.)

The radicals endeavor to smooth the hideous visage of this reconstruction by asserting that it is indispensable to prevent the Democracy getting power and repudiating the National debt. In other words, to prevent repudiation, some device must be arranged by which a majority of the legal electors of ten states shall not be permitted to rule them. If that necessity really exists, the dire event can not be long postponed by devising in the interest of the national creditors, a scheme of reconstruction which violates the Constitution and the fundamental theory of our government;

breaks pledges of infinitely more sacred obligation than the money debt; cripples every industry of the land, and while reducing one-half every man's ability to pay taxes, doubles his share of the public burden—the essential condition of which scheme is to the perpetuation of the rule of a party which now represents not one-third of the white people of the nation. But, thank God, that necessity does not exist! The credit of the Republic, as the union of the States, rests secure *in the hearts of the people.* (Applause.) A vast majority of all parties will preserve and defend it, as they did the Union. But if the national credit could be shaken, it would be by the public creditors flocking into one party, and, under the panoply of the national honor, scheming to perpetuate the power of that party at the cost of the established Constitutions and liberties of the States and the nation. (Great applause—cries of "That's so.")

To accomplish this scheme of reconstruction, the Constitution is not only abrogated so far as the Southern States are concerned, but the form of our government is being destroyed by the absorption by Congress of the chief powers of the National Executive:

Congress has assumed to take from the President the control of the army which the Constitution gives him, and to commit that part of it employed in the South to General Grant and five district commanders (hisses), independent of the orders of the President. By this bold assumption of power, it has converted many high officers of the regular army to radicalism, and made them zealous instruments of its usurpations.

It has usurped the pardoning power, which the Constitution gives solely to the President, and by sweeping bills of pains and penalties, proscribed the intelligent white men of the South, notwithstanding the pardons of the President. And it now shamelessly avows that it will give *congressional pardon* only to those who eat the leek of radicalism. (Hisses.)

All such are *loyal*, though, like Governor Brown, of Georgia, they drove and dragged their people into rebellion, and, coward-like, seized our arsenals and navy yards while yet wearing the mask of loyalty; while men like George W. Jones, of Tennessee, who stood by the Union from the first, but who opposed negro suffrage and white disfranchisement, are stigmatized as "*heart malignants*," deserving only proscription at the hands of the Sumners, and Kellys, and Butlers of Congress—(Great hisses. Cries, " Who stole the spoons?" " Dutch Gap.")

" Those pseudo privy-councilors of God,
Who write down judgments with a pen hard-nibbed."

It took, too, from the President, the power of removal, thus fomenting insubordination in the civil service as it had done in the military—prohibiting even the removal of his own cabinet officers, the adjutants through whom he gives orders and receives reports.

And it crowned its usurpations by an impeachment founded on a statute it had passed, enacting the glaring and flagitious lie that it is a high crime for the President to discharge the duties of removal imposed on him by the Constitution, as interpreted by the uniform usage of government from the administration of Washington down (applause); or even to so far attempt to exercise it, as to bring the question of his Constitutional power of removal to decision by the Supreme Court—that high arbiter fixed by the Constitution to settle every conflict over boundaries of power between the States and the United States, or between departments of the general government. And, after having impeached him, and while giving him a lynch-law trial, the party, with a ferocity unparalleled even in the violent controversies of the day, brought its almost irresistible power to bear through its leading men, its press, and its conventions, to force Republican Senators to commit moral perjury by an insincere verdict. So foul an act was never before attempted by a party in this nation.

Had Andrew Johnson consulted his own interests, and become the instrument of a lawless faction, these essential executive powers would not have been disturbed, nor he arraigned as a criminal at the bar of the Senate. But, to his eternal renown (applause), he stood by the Constitution when it was assailed by his party, as boldly and grandly as he had stood by the Union when the storm of war burst over and around it:

> "Unshaken, unseduced, unterrified,
> His loyalty he kept, his love, his zeal;
> Nor number nor example with him wrought,
> To swerve from truth or change his constant mind."

[Three cheers for Andrew Johnson. Three cheers for President Johnson. Tumultuous cheering.]

Gentlemen, in any government but ours, usurpations so flagrant and fundamental would result in revolution; in ours they can be overthrown by the people at the ballot box. The appeal to the people this fall will decide whether the radicals shall retain or surrender the power they have thus used, and are using, for the destruction of the Union and of our form of National Government.

If we could so take our appeal as to present to the people the living issues between the parties free from the rubbish of past issues, who could doubt the result? If the Democracy could give us a candidate who would unite as thoroughly the opponents of radical rule as General Grant unites its supporters, that candidate would carry nine-tenths of the electoral college. (Applause.) The strength of the radicals is not in their cause, but in the divisions of their adversaries.

The war was a success—not a failure. It settled the theretofore disputed and doubtful question of secession against the right to secede. It settled, too, the subject of slavery. (Applause.) These, however, were unsettled questions in 1864, and were thought to be involved in the political contest of that year. Now, the passions of the war and of that political controversy are not as dead as these issues in which they played their part. From them came all the hopes of the radicals, and all the fears of the friends of the Constitution and the Union. Rousing these slumbering passions of the war, and led on by one of its foremost generals, the radicals hope to fight over again the political battle of 1864. Shall they do it? ("No, no.") Ah, gentlemen, I wish this convention could decide that question—but it is for the Democratic Convention to decide. By its choice of leader it will determine the battle-ground, and decide whether the Democracy shall triumph on living issues or be routed on dead ones (Applause); *whether the radicals shall be arraigned and tried for what they are doing, or the Democracy, for what they did or failed to do four years ago?*

Of a million and a half of present voters who served in the Union army or navy, this Convention represents at least a half. (Voices, "More than one-half," "Two-thirds," "Three-fourths.") Of these so represented, a half or more (among whom I wish to be reckoned as one) will support any of the Democrats whose names have been mentioned for the Presidency; but the remainder, numbering several hundred thousand voters, will be won or lost to the cause, as the nomination proves wise or *otherwise*. (Laughter and applause.) This Convention has assembled in no spirit of dictation, but animated by devotion to the Constitution and the Union, and kindness to all who would preserve them, to aid in securing an harmonious nomination, and organizing a certain victory. I can not suffer myself to doubt that the Democratic party has assembled this day in the same patriotic spirit, and will present a candidate who, whether he fought for the Union or not, thoroughly sustained the war (great applause), and whom all the soldiers and sailors of the Union can support without even seeming inconsistency.

The Republican party represents no principle for which we fought. We thought not of negro suffrage (applause and cries of "No, no"), or of white disfranchisement; of forcing on the Southern States unequal fellowship in the Union ("Never, never"), of changing our beneficent form of government ("No, never"), or of perpetuating the Republican party ("Never, never"). Out of the five hundred thousand of Union soldiers, Democrats and Republicans, who sleep on fields washed by the waters of the Atlantic and the Gulf, not one laid down his life for any such end. Of the fifteen hundred thousand of their surviving comrades, not one will say he would have risked his life for either of these objects. And these measures of the Republican party are not only not the objects of the war, but are so prosecuted as to defeat those objects, and to inflict on the nation evils as great as those the war was waged to prevent. (Shouts, "That's so.")

The Democratic party is now the only party true to the Constitution and the Union. (Applause.) If we would accomplish the purposes of our service and sacrifice, if we would save the Union, the States, their liberties, and laws, we must unite with the Democracy. (Long continued applause.) We must not ask what men *have been*, but what they *are*; not who *lately* defended the Constitution, but who *now* defend it. (Great applause.) In the path which the Democratic party treads, we see the footprints of Washington, Jefferson, Madison, Adams, and all the heroes of the revolution; of Webster, Jackson, Clay, Wright, and all the giants of the generation just gone before us; and while it keeps that line of march, and bears the flag of the Constitution and the Union, we can follow it with pride and with unfaltering trust. (Immense applause, cheers, and waving of hats, followed by the band playing "Rally round the flag.")

www.ingramcontent.com/pod-product-compliance
Lightning Source LLC
Chambersburg PA
CBHW022002100426
42738CB00042B/1386